POWER OF SILENCE

(Unleashing the Power Within)

MEERA

Power of Silence

(Unleashing the Power Within)

BY

Meera

ISBN: 978-93-95773-54-6

Published by RIGI PUBLICATION

777, Street no.9, Krishna Nagar

Khanna-141401 (Punjab), India

Website: www.rigipublication.com

Email: info@rigipublication.com

Phone: +91-9357710014, +91-9465468291

INTRODUCTION

- **Embracing the Potential of Silence:**

In a world filled with constant noise and distractions, finding moments of silence can seem elusive. Yet, within the hushed stillness lies a profound potential waiting to be discovered. It is in these moments of silence that we can connect with our innermost selves, tap into our innate wisdom, and unlock a power that resides within each of us.

This book is an exploration of the transformative power of silence and an invitation to embrace its potential. Silence is not merely the absence of sound; it is a doorway to self-discovery, healing, creativity, and spiritual connection. It is a tool that allows us to pause, reflect, and cultivate a deeper awareness of ourselves and the world around us.

In the following chapters, we will delve into various aspects of silence and its impact on our lives. We will uncover the art of listening deeply, both to ourselves and to others, and discover how silence can enhance our communication and relationships. We will also explore how silence can serve as a catalyst for healing, providing solace and rejuvenation amidst the chaos of daily life.

Silence is not about withdrawing from the world; rather, it is about creating an inner sanctuary where we can find respite and nourishment for our souls. Through mindfulness practices, we can learn to harness the power of silence to cultivate self-awareness, enhance our focus, and tap into our inner power and resilience.

Moreover, silence can ignite our creativity, opening doors to inspiration and innovation that lie dormant within us. We will explore how silence can provide the fertile ground for ideas to flourish and how it can deepen our connection to our intuition, guiding us on our unique paths.

Ultimately, this book invites you to embark on a journey of self-discovery and growth through the power of silence. It is an invitation to slow down, embrace the moments of quietude, and unlock the treasures that lie within. By embracing silence, we can unleash our full potential, live more authentically, and cultivate a profound sense of inner peace and fulfillment.

So, let us embark on this journey together, as we delve into the transformative power of silence and uncover the hidden gems that await us in the depths of stillness. Get ready to embrace the potential of silence and unlock the power that resides within you.

INDEX

Chapter 1: The Essence of Silence

Silence, often overlooked in a world filled with noise, holds a profound essence that has the power to transform our lives. It is in the moments of quietude that we can truly connect with our inner selves and experience the depth of our being.

In this chapter, we delve into the true essence of silence. We explore how silence is not simply the absence of noise, but a space of infinite possibilities. It is a canvas upon which our thoughts, emotions, and experiences can unfold with clarity and grace.

By embracing silence, we invite a sense of stillness into our lives, allowing us to detach from the external chaos and turn inward. It is in this stillness that we discover a profound sense of peace, tranquility, and connection to our innermost selves.

We explore the power of silence in providing a sanctuary for self-reflection and self-discovery. In the absence of distractions, we gain clarity and insight into our thoughts, feelings, and desires. We begin to discern the essence of who we truly are, free from the external influences and societal expectations.

Moreover, we uncover how silence can be a powerful source of inspiration and creativity. It is in the quiet moments that our minds become open and receptive to new ideas, insights, and breakthroughs. Silence allows our inner wisdom to speak and guide us on our creative journeys.

Through various practices and techniques, we can cultivate the art of silence in our daily lives. We learn to embrace silence as a nourishing force that revitalizes our energy, restores balance, and enhances our overall well-being.

In this chapter, we invite you to explore the essence of silence and its profound impact on your life. Discover the transformative power of silence as you embark on a journey of self-discovery, inspiration, and inner peace. Open yourself to the possibilities that arise in the moments of stillness and experience the true essence of silence within you.

1.1 Exploring the profound nature of silence

Silence is a concept that holds deep and profound meaning across various aspects of human experience, philosophy, and spirituality. Here are some perspectives on the profound nature of silence:

Inner Reflection and Mindfulness:

Silence provides an opportunity for inner reflection and mindfulness. In a world filled with constant noise and distractions, moments of silence allow us to turn inward, observe our thoughts, and gain a deeper understanding of ourselves. It can lead to increased self-awareness, emotional regulation, and mental clarity.

Communication beyond Words:

Silence can convey meaning and emotions that words often struggle to express. It can communicate a range of feelings, from peace and contentment to sadness and reverence. Sometimes, the most profound connections with others can occur in shared moments of silence.

Stillness and Presence:

Silence is closely related to stillness and presence. By quieting external and internal noise, we can be fully present in the moment. This can enhance our ability to appreciate the beauty of the world around us and engage more deeply with our surroundings.

Creativity and Inspiration:

Silence can be a fertile ground for creativity and inspiration. Many artists, writers, and thinkers find that moments of quiet contemplation help they tap into their creative wellsprings. In the absence of external distractions, the mind is free to wander and make unexpected connections.

Spiritual and Transcendent Experience:

Silence holds significance in various spiritual and religious traditions. It is often associated with a connection to the divine or the universe. Practices like meditation, prayer, and mindfulness involve seeking profound experiences through silence and inner stillness.

Mystery and Depth:

Silence can evoke a sense of mystery and depth. It reminds us that there are aspects of existence that may elude verbal description or logical explanation. In this way, silence can open the door to contemplation of life's fundamental questions and mysteries.

Respect and Reverence:

Silence is often observed in moments of respect and reverence. It's used during ceremonies, rituals, and memorials to convey a deep sense of honor and solemnity. In these contexts, silence speaks volumes about the significance of the event or person being commemorated.

Healing and Restoration:

Silence can offer a space for healing and restoration. Taking time away from noise and chaos can provide a soothing and rejuvenating effect on the mind and body. Silence can help reduce stress, improve sleep, and promote overall well-being.

In exploring the profound nature of silence, it's important to recognize that silence can have different meanings and impacts for each individual. What might be a deeply meaningful experience of silence for one person could differ for another. Embracing moments of silence and integrating them into our lives can lead to a deeper understanding of ourselves, our surroundings, and the mysteries of existence

1.2 Transformative power of silence

The transformative power of silence is an awe-inspiring force that unfolds in the quiet spaces of our lives. It holds the potential to reshape our thoughts, emotions, and perspectives, offering a profound journey of self-discovery and growth.

In the midst of a world brimming with constant noise and distractions, silence serves as a sanctuary where we can recalibrate our internal compass. Through introspection and mindfulness, we navigate the depths of our own minds, unearthing insights that might have remained hidden amid the din of everyday life. This self-imposed pause allows us to understand our desires, fears, and motivations with a clarity that noisy surroundings often obscure.

Silence is a catalyst for creativity, acting as a blank canvas upon which our imaginations can paint vibrant tapestries. It invites us to explore the uncharted territories of our thoughts, fostering connections between ideas that might have remained unlinked in the bustling world. In this fertile ground, the seeds of innovation take root, and groundbreaking ideas flourish.

At its core, silence is a doorway to spiritual exploration and transformation. Through practices like meditation and contemplation, we transcend the limitations of the material world and connect with something greater than ourselves. Silence becomes a vessel through which we commune with the universe, experiencing a sense of interconnectedness and finding answers to life's most profound questions.

In relationships, silence holds a unique power to foster deeper connections. In shared moments of quietude, unspoken emotions are exchanged, and unbreakable bonds are formed. The absence of words can often convey more than a thousand sentences, revealing empathy, understanding, and shared experiences that strengthen relationships.

However, harnessing the transformative power of silence requires intentional practice. It demands that we embrace the discomfort of facing ourselves without distractions and confront our thoughts, both pleasant and uncomfortable. It asks us to let go of our impulse to fill every moment with noise, instead allowing space for the wisdom that silence brings.

As we surrender to the silence, we emerge transformed. We shed old habits, gain new perspectives, and evolve into versions of ourselves that are more aligned with our true essence. The transformative power of silence is an invitation to journey inward, to listen to the whispers of our hearts, and to emerge from the cocoon of quietude with newfound clarity, purpose, and a profound understanding of the symphony of existence.

Chapter 2: The Inner Sanctuary

Within the busyness of our lives, there exists a secret space—an inner sanctuary where we can find peace and rejuvenation. This sanctuary is not bound by physical walls but resides within us, waiting to be discovered.

In this chapter, we explore the concept of the inner sanctuary—a refuge from the noise and chaos of the world. It is a place where we can detach from external demands and reconnect with our true selves.

Through practices like meditation and mindfulness, we learn to access this sanctuary. By closing our eyes and focusing on our breath, we create a sacred space within, free from distractions. In this inner sanctuary, we experience a sense of calmness and centeredness.

The inner sanctuary is where self-reflection and self-discovery thrive. Here, we can explore our thoughts and emotions, gaining clarity and insight. It is a space for nurturing our dreams, desires, and passions.

Moreover, the inner sanctuary is a place of healing and rejuvenation. Within its embrace, we can release stress, anxiety, and negativity. It is a sanctuary where we can replenish our energy and find solace amidst life's challenges.

As we cultivate our inner sanctuary, we tap into a wellspring of inspiration and creativity. Ideas flow effortlessly, and our intuition guides us towards new possibilities. It is within this space that our true potential can be unleashed.

The inner sanctuary is always accessible, and we carry it within us wherever we go. It is a sanctuary that empowers us to face the world with grace, resilience, and a deeper sense of self-awareness.

In this chapter, we invite you to discover and nurture your own inner sanctuary. Through simple practices and intentional moments of stillness, you can tap into the transformative power it holds. Embrace the sanctuary within, and unlock a source of peace, clarity, and personal growth in your life.

2.1 Creating a Sacred Space for Silence and Introspection:

In the midst of our bustling lives, it is essential to carve out a sacred space where silence and introspection can thrive. This space becomes a sanctuary—a place where we can retreat, reconnect with ourselves, and nourish our souls.

Creating this sacred space starts with setting aside a physical environment that promotes stillness and tranquility. It can be a cozy corner in your home, a serene garden, or a quiet room where you can immerse yourself in silence. Clear away clutter, add elements that bring you peace (such as candles, cushions, or soothing artwork), and make it a dedicated space for introspection.

Once the physical space is prepared, it's time to create an atmosphere conducive to silence and introspection. This can involve turning off distractions like electronic devices or playing soft, ambient music that helps you relax. Cultivate an environment that encourages you to disconnect from the external noise and connect with your inner self.

With the outer space ready, shift your attention to your inner state. Settle into the sacred space and bring your awareness to the present moment. Close your eyes, take deep breaths, and allow the outside world to fade away. Embrace silence as a companion, a guide to introspection.

Within this sacred space, invite yourself to explore the depths of your being. Reflect on your thoughts, emotions, and experiences without judgment or attachment. This is a space for deep self-inquiry, where you can ask yourself meaningful questions and listen to the whispers of your heart.

As you spend time in this sacred space, you may discover insights, clarity, and a sense of connection with your true essence. It is a sanctuary for self-discovery, self-compassion, and self-growth.

Creating a sacred space for silence and introspection is an intentional act of self-care. It is a gift you give yourself—a refuge where you can find solace, cultivate inner peace, and nurture your well-being.

In this chapter, we invite you to embark on the journey of creating your own sacred space. Discover the power of silence and introspection, and witness the profound transformations that unfold when you create a sanctuary for your inner self.

2.2 Cultivating inner stillness amidst the noise of everyday life:

Breathing Anchors:

Inhale. Exhale. Take a moment to focus on your breath. Amidst the noise of daily life, use your breath as an anchor to cultivate inner stillness. By consciously returning to the rhythm of your breath, you can find moments of calm amidst the chaos.

Mindful Pauses:

In the midst of a hectic day, pause for a moment. Close your eyes, take a deep breath, and tune in to your present experience. Allow the noise around you to fade into the background as you reconnect with your inner stillness. These mindful pauses offer a sanctuary of tranquility.

Nature's Embrace:

Escape the noise by immersing yourself in nature. Find a peaceful spot—whether it's a park, garden, or even your backyard—and allow the sights, sounds, and sensations of nature to wash over you. Let the gentle rustling of leaves and the melodies of birds restore your inner stillness.

Silent Rituals:

Incorporate moments of silence into your daily routines. Whether it's during your morning coffee, a walk, or even while doing household chores, intentionally embrace the silence. By savoring these silent rituals, you create space for inner stillness to blossom amidst the hustle and bustle.

Digital Detox:

Unplug from the constant noise of technology. Designate tech-free periods or spaces, allowing yourself to disconnect from screens and immerse in quietude. Embracing a digital detox nurtures a peaceful mind and fosters the cultivation of inner stillness.

These practices offer simple yet powerful ways to cultivate inner stillness amidst the noise of everyday life. By incorporating them into your routine, you create moments of tranquility and rediscover the peace that resides within, enabling you to navigate life's challenges with grace and clarity.

Chapter 3: The Language of Silence

Silence has a language all its own—one that transcends words and reaches the depths of understanding. In this chapter, we delve into the significance of the language of silence and its impact on our connections and communication.

Within the realm of silence, we discover the power of deep listening. By quieting our inner chatter and truly focusing on others, we create space for genuine understanding and empathy. The language of silence allows us to listen with our hearts and connect on a profound level.

Non-verbal communication plays a vital role in the language of silence. Through facial expressions, gestures, and subtle cues, we convey emotions and meaning that words may struggle to capture. Embracing the power of silence as a mode of expression enhances our ability to communicate authentically and intuitively.

Silence also empowers us to respond instead of react. By pausing and embracing the stillness within, we can choose our words and actions more mindfully. This intentional silence fosters harmony and resolution, transforming conflict into compassionate dialogue.

The language of silence extends beyond our interactions with others—it speaks to our relationship with ourselves. In moments of quiet reflection, we gain insights into our thoughts, emotions, and desires. Silence becomes a guide in self-discovery, enabling us to live in alignment with our authentic selves.

This chapter invites you to explore the language of silence and its transformative potential. By embracing silence as a mode of communication, both in your interactions with others and in your inner dialogue, you unlock a profound language that fosters connection, empathy, and self-awareness.

The Healing Silence:

Sarah, a close friend, opens up about her recent struggles with anxiety. Instead of offering advice or trying to fix the problem, Emma sits in silence, holding a safe space for Sarah to express herself fully. Through her attentive presence, Emma allows Sarah to feel heard, understood, and supported without judgment. In this silence, their connection deepens, and Sarah finds solace in being truly listened to and understood.

The Unspoken Understanding:

In a quiet moment, a couple, Lisa and Mark, sit together, silently holding hands. They have had a long, exhausting day, filled with responsibilities and demands. In this shared silence, they feel a profound connection—a wordless understanding of each other's fatigue, hopes, and dreams. Without uttering a single word, they find comfort and strength in knowing they are there for each other, silently supporting one another through the ups and downs of life.

The Silent Reflection:

During a team meeting, Mark shares a challenging idea, unsure of how it will be received. Instead of immediately jumping in with opinions, the team members take a moment of silence to reflect. Each person pauses to fully understand and process Mark's perspective. Through this shared silence, they create space for deeper insights and a more thoughtful, collaborative discussion. The silence fosters an environment of mutual respect and allows everyone's voice to be heard.

The Empathetic Pause:

Alice, a counselor, sits with a grieving client, John, who recently lost a loved one. Instead of filling the session with words, Alice offers compassionate silence, allowing John to express his emotions at his own pace. Through this empathetic pause, John feels validated and understood, as if his pain is being acknowledged without the need for words. In the silence, a profound connection is established, supporting John on his journey of healing.

These examples demonstrate the transformative power of deep listening and connecting with others on a profound level. By embracing the language of silence, we can foster understanding, compassion, and authentic connections in our relationships, creating spaces where others feel seen, heard, and valued.

Chapter 4: Silence and Mindfulness

Silence and mindfulness are two concepts that are often interconnected and can be beneficial for one's mental well-being. Let's explore each of them individually and their potential relationship.

Silence:

Silence refers to the absence of noise, speech, or external distractions. In today's fast-paced and noisy world, finding moments of silence can be challenging but incredibly valuable. Silence provides an opportunity to calm the mind, reduce stress, and promote a sense of inner peace. It allows us to disconnect from the constant influx of information and stimuli and create space for reflection and introspection. Silence can be experienced through solitude, meditation, nature walks, or simply finding quiet corners in our daily lives.

Mindfulness:

Mindfulness, on the other hand, is a mental state of being fully present and engaged in the current moment, without judgment or attachment. It involves intentionally paying attention to our thoughts, feelings, bodily sensations, and the surrounding environment. Mindfulness can be cultivated through various practices such as meditation, deep breathing exercises, or even mundane activities like washing dishes or walking. By practicing mindfulness, we develop an enhanced awareness of our experiences, which allows us to respond to them with greater clarity, compassion, and resilience.

4.1 Harnessing the Benefits of Mindfulness Meditation:

Mindfulness meditation, with its deep-rooted traditions and scientifically proven benefits, has emerged as a transformative practice in our fast-paced, stress-laden lives. At its core, mindfulness meditation invites us to embrace the present moment with open curiosity and non-judgmental awareness. By cultivating this intentional focus and redirecting our attention away from past regrets or future anxieties, we unlock a wealth of benefits that extend far beyond the meditation cushion.

One of the key rewards of mindfulness meditation lies in its ability to calm the incessant chatter of our minds. As we settle into the practice, we learn to observe our thoughts and emotions without being carried away by them. This heightened self-awareness allows us to identify negative thought patterns, self-limiting beliefs, and unhelpful reactions that might have once held us captive. With gentle and compassionate exploration, we begin to untangle ourselves from the grip of these mental patterns, opening up a new space for clarity and wise decision-making.

Moreover, mindfulness meditation holds the power to liberate us from the shackles of stress and anxiety. By anchoring our attention to the present moment, we detach ourselves from the burdensome weight of past regrets or future worries. This shift in perspective enables us to break free from the cycle of stress and cultivate a greater sense of calm and inner peace. Through regular practice, we strengthen our resilience and develop an inner sanctuary where we can retreat in times of turbulence, finding solace and stability amidst life's inevitable storms.

Beyond mental and emotional well-being, mindfulness meditation has shown promising effects on our physical health. Studies have indicated that this practice can lower blood pressure, reduce chronic pain, and boost the immune system. By cultivating mindfulness, we tap into the mind-body connection and initiate a profound healing process within ourselves. With each mindful breath, we nourish our bodies and create an environment that supports optimal well-being.

Perhaps one of the most remarkable aspects of mindfulness meditation is its potential for self-transformation. As we become attuned to the present moment, we start to develop a profound sense of compassion and acceptance towards ourselves and others. This shift in perspective opens the doors to enhanced self-compassion, empathy, and deeper connections with those around us. Mindfulness meditation becomes a vehicle for personal growth, enabling us to shed layers of conditioning, awaken our innate wisdom, and live with authenticity and purpose.

In harnessing the benefits of mindfulness meditation, we embark on a lifelong journey of self-discovery and self-care. Through dedicated practice, we learn to befriend ourselves, cultivate resilience, and nourish our overall well-being. By embracing the present moment and stepping into the transformative power of mindfulness, we unlock the keys to living a more fulfilling, connected, and balanced life.

4.2 Using Silence as a Tool for Self-Awareness and Presence:

Silence, often overlooked in our noisy and fast-paced world, holds a profound capacity to cultivate self-awareness and deepen our sense of presence. By intentionally embracing moments of silence, we create a space for reflection, introspection, and heightened consciousness. It is in this tranquil void that we can truly listen to ourselves, tune into our inner voice, and develop a profound understanding of our thoughts, emotions, and desires.

Imagine a busy executive who finds solace in a daily practice of silence. In the early morning hours, before the world awakens, she carves out a sacred space for silence. As she sits in stillness, the external noise fades away, allowing her to turn inward and attune to the rhythm of her breath. In this silence, she becomes acutely aware of her racing thoughts, the weight of stress in her body, and the subtle nuances of her emotions. With gentle observation and non-judgmental awareness, she acknowledges and releases the mental and emotional burdens that have accumulated over time.

Through the practice of silence, she develops a greater sense of self-awareness. She recognizes the patterns and triggers that shape her reactions and behaviors. In this stillness, she is able to discern between the authentic voice of her intuition and the loud echoes of societal expectations. This heightened self-awareness becomes a compass guiding her decisions and actions, enabling her to align with her values and live a more authentic and fulfilling life.

Silence also serves as a gateway to deepening presence. In a world that constantly demands our attention, the practice of silence allows us to fully immerse ourselves in the present moment. As we release the distractions and external stimuli, we open ourselves to the richness of our immediate surroundings. We become attuned to the beauty of nature, the subtleties of human interaction, and the wonders of our own existence. Through silence, we embrace the fullness of the present moment, infusing it with our undivided attention and genuine presence.

By utilizing silence as a tool for self-awareness and presence, we create a foundation for personal growth, inner peace, and meaningful connection with ourselves and others. Whether it's through moments of silent meditation, mindful walks in nature, or simply pausing amidst the busyness of everyday life, silence offers us a profound opportunity to recharge, recalibrate, and come home to ourselves. In this hallowed stillness, we uncover the depth of our being and rediscover the innate wisdom that resides within.

Chapter 5: Silence and Healing

Silence holds a profound capacity to nurture and facilitate the healing process. In the stillness of silence, we create an environment of calm and serenity that allows for deep introspection and self-reflection. It is within this tranquil space that healing can take place on multiple levels - physically, emotionally, and spiritually. Silence invites us to let go of the external noise and distractions, turning our attention inward to listen to the whispers of our inner selves. In this sacred silence, we find solace, clarity, and the opportunity to release emotional burdens, process trauma, and nurture our overall well-being. By embracing silence as a healing tool, we embark on a transformative journey of self-discovery, restoration, and a renewed sense of wholeness.

5.1 Exploring the Therapeutic Aspects of Silence:

Silence, often overlooked in a world filled with constant noise and stimulation, possesses profound therapeutic qualities that can benefit our mental, emotional, and physical well-being. In the absence of external distractions, silence becomes a sacred space where we can turn inward and attune to the subtle nuances of our inner landscape. Within this tranquil refuge, we discover the power of self-reflection, self-awareness, and self-discovery. Silence allows us to observe our thoughts, emotions, and sensations with a gentle curiosity, fostering a deeper understanding of ourselves and our experiences. It offers a respite from the relentless demands of modern life, providing an opportunity to recharge, recalibrate, and find inner peace. In the therapeutic embrace of silence, we can heal past wounds, find clarity amidst chaos, and cultivate a sense of wholeness and balance. Silence becomes a guiding companion on our journey of self-exploration, facilitating personal growth, emotional resilience, and a profound connection with our authentic selves.

5.2 Using Silence as a Catalyst for Emotional and Physical Well-being:

Silence, often underestimated and overshadowed by the noise of daily life, possesses an extraordinary power to serve as a catalyst for our emotional and physical well-being. Within the gentle embrace of silence, we can find profound healing, restoration, and transformation. By intentionally immersing ourselves in moments of stillness, we unlock the hidden potential to nurture our emotional landscape and enhance our overall health.

Emotionally, silence acts as a sanctuary for reflection, offering us a precious opportunity to delve into the depths of our feelings and thoughts. As we embrace silence, we invite a sense of calm and spaciousness that allows buried emotions to rise to the surface. In the absence of distractions, we can courageously face our inner world, process unresolved emotions, and offer ourselves the compassion and self-care we truly deserve. Silence becomes a catalyst for emotional healing, granting us the necessary space to release emotional burdens, find clarity, and restore balance within ourselves.

Moreover, silence fosters mindfulness and presence, enabling us to cultivate a deep connection with the present moment. As we immerse ourselves in silence, we become attuned to the subtleties of our physical sensations, our breath, and the rhythms of our bodies. In this heightened state of awareness, we tap into the innate wisdom of our physical being, allowing our bodies to communicate their needs and restore their natural state of well-being. Silence serves as a catalyst for physical healing, creating an environment where we can recharge, rejuvenate, and support the body's natural ability to heal itself.

In the realm of emotional and physical well-being, silence acts as a gateway to self-care and self-discovery. It invites us to cultivate a compassionate and nurturing relationship with ourselves, where we prioritize moments of silence as essential components of our daily routines. Through the practice of silence, we deepen our self-awareness, develop resilience, and gain insight into the interconnectedness of our emotional and physical well-being.

By consciously integrating silence into our lives, we honor the wisdom that resides within us and align ourselves with the harmonious rhythms of the universe. Whether through silent meditation, nature walks, or simply finding pockets of quiet in our daily lives, we can harness the transformative power of silence to nurture our emotional landscape, support our physical well-being, and create a foundation for overall health and vitality.

In this fast-paced world, let us remember the immense value of silence as a catalyst for our emotional and physical well-being. Let us embrace moments of stillness, allowing the profound healing power of silence to guide us on a transformative journey toward wholeness, presence, and a more vibrant and balanced life.

Chapter 6: Silence and Intuition

Silence serves as the sacred ground upon which our intuition can flourish and speak with clarity. In the absence of noise and distractions, we create a space where the whispers of our inner wisdom can be heard. It is within the profound silence that we can access the depths of our intuition, that inner compass guiding us towards our authentic path.

When we embrace silence, we invite a state of receptivity, attuning our senses to the subtle messages that arise from within. In the hushed stillness, our intuition speaks through whispers, nudges, and gut feelings. It is a language that bypasses the noise of the rational mind, offering profound insights and guidance that may otherwise go unnoticed.

Silence provides a refuge from the constant external influences that can cloud our judgment and sway our decisions. In the quietude, we can discern the difference between the noise of external expectations and the gentle nudges of our intuition. We become attuned to the authentic voice within, offering clarity, wisdom, and a deep sense of knowing.

As we cultivate a regular practice of silence, we strengthen the connection to our intuition. We learn to trust the quiet nudges that arise, even when they defy logic or societal norms. Through silence, we tap into the wellspring of innate wisdom that resides within us, empowering us to make choices aligned with our deepest values and desires.

Silence and intuition go hand in hand, as the stillness of the mind allows the intuitive voice to rise to the surface. In this symbiotic relationship, silence nurtures our intuition, while intuition illuminates the path within silence. They form a harmonious dance that guides us towards greater self-awareness, authenticity, and fulfillment.

Let us honor the power of silence as a sacred space for deepening our connection with our intuition. By embracing moments of quiet contemplation, meditation, and inner reflection, we cultivate a fertile ground for our intuition to blossom. In the gentle embrace of silence, we unlock the innate wisdom that resides within us, allowing our intuition to guide us towards a life infused with purpose, meaning, and alignment with our true selves

6.1 Cultivating Intuition through Moments of Silence:

Moments of silence offer us a precious opportunity to cultivate and deepen our intuition, that innate and powerful guidance system within us. When we intentionally carve out space for silence, we create a fertile ground for our intuition to thrive and blossom.

In the stillness of silence, we invite a heightened state of presence and attunement. As the external noise fades away, we become more receptive to the subtle whispers of our intuition. In this receptive state, we can listen deeply to the wisdom that arises from within, allowing our intuition to guide us towards what feels true, authentic, and aligned.

Through regular practice, we strengthen our connection to our intuition. By embracing moments of silence, whether through meditation, contemplation, or simply being present in the stillness of nature, we create a nurturing environment for our intuition to flourish. We become more attuned to the sensations, emotions, and insights that arise, learning to trust the intuitive nudges that guide us towards clarity and wise decision-making.

Silence serves as a sanctuary for the cultivation of intuition. It provides a respite from the noise and distractions of the external world, allowing us to tune into the subtleties of our inner world. In this sanctuary, we can reflect on our experiences, gain deeper self-awareness, and access the wisdom that resides within us. Through silence, we become better acquainted with our intuitive voice, learning to distinguish it from the clamor of our thoughts and external influences.

As we integrate moments of silence into our daily lives, we develop a profound trust in our intuition. We recognize that it is a reliable compass, offering guidance beyond what can be reasoned or explained. In the silence, we learn to surrender to the intuitive whispers, even when they may challenge our logical mind or societal expectations. We cultivate the courage to follow our intuitive guidance, knowing that it leads us towards our highest good and authentic path.

By intentionally nurturing our intuition through moments of silence, we tap into a wellspring of wisdom, creativity, and insight. We access a deeper level of knowing, allowing us to navigate life with greater clarity, purpose, and alignment. In the sanctuary of silence, we discover that our intuition is a trusted ally, guiding us towards a life that resonates with our true selves.

Let us embrace the transformative power of silence, cherishing and cultivating moments of stillness as a pathway to deepen our connection to our intuition. Through the gentle practice of silence, we unlock the profound guidance that resides within us, enabling us to navigate our journey with grace, trust, and a profound sense of inner knowing.

6.2 Trusting the Wisdom That Arises in the Stillness:

Laura, a successful corporate executive, found herself feeling burnt out and disconnected from her true passions. Seeking guidance, she turned to moments of stillness as a way to reconnect with her inner wisdom and regain a sense of purpose. Each morning, she dedicated time to sit in silence, allowing herself to fully embrace the present moment.

In the quiet sanctuary of her meditation practice, Laura began to notice subtle whispers of intuition rising to the surface. Ideas, inspirations, and insights that had previously been drowned out by the noise of her busy life now emerged with clarity and strength. She felt a deep sense of trust in the wisdom that arose in those moments of stillness.

One morning, during her silent contemplation, Laura received a profound intuitive message. It was a calling to pursue a new career path, one aligned with her true passions and values. Initially, doubt and fear tried to cloud her judgment, questioning the feasibility and practicality of such a change. However, she chose to trust the wisdom that had arisen in the stillness.

Embracing her intuition, Laura took inspired action, gradually transitioning into a new career that aligned with her deepest aspirations. It was not an easy journey, but the trust she had cultivated in the wisdom of silence carried her forward. As she navigated the challenges and uncertainties, she discovered a newfound resilience and inner strength that supported her every step of the way.

Trusting the wisdom that arose in the stillness became a guiding principle in Laura's life. As she continued to cultivate moments of silence and self-reflection, her intuition served as a compass, offering guidance and clarity in both personal and professional decisions. She witnessed the transformative power of embracing those intuitive nudges, leading her towards a life filled with purpose, fulfillment, and authentic expression.

Laura's story is a testament to the transformative potential of trusting the wisdom that arises in the stillness. Through her practice of silence, she learned to quiet the noise of doubt and external expectations, allowing her intuition to take center stage. By cultivating trust in the insights that emerged during those moments of stillness, Laura embraced a life guided by her inner wisdom, and in doing so, she found the fulfillment and alignment she had been seeking

Chapter 7: Silence and Creativity

Silence serves as a fertile ground where creativity can flourish and new ideas can emerge. In the absence of external noise and distractions, we create a space for our imagination to roam freely and for inspiration to arise organically. Embracing moments of silence allows us to tap into the vast reservoirs of creativity within us, opening the door to innovative thinking, artistic expression, and transformative ideas.

In the sanctuary of silence, we quiet the incessant chatter of our minds, creating a receptive space for fresh insights and connections to form. As we immerse ourselves in the stillness, our thoughts settle, and we become more attuned to the subtle whispers of our inner muse. In this receptive state, we unlock new perspectives, alternative solutions, and innovative approaches to creative challenges.

Silence invites us to engage in deep reflection, introspection, and self-discovery. As we tune out external stimuli, we turn our attention inward, exploring the vast landscapes of our inner world. It is within this exploration that we encounter our unique stories, passions, and dreams, igniting the spark of creativity within us. The silence becomes a canvas on which we can paint our thoughts, ideas, and artistic visions with clarity and authenticity.

Moreover, silence provides a nurturing environment for creative incubation and incubation. In the absence of noise and distractions, we give ourselves permission to be still, allowing ideas to gestate and evolve naturally. As we surrender to the creative flow that emerges from the silence, we unlock a wellspring of inspiration, originality, and artistic expression that can transform our work and leave a lasting impact.

Silence and creativity share a symbiotic relationship, as silence enhances creativity, and creativity enriches the silence. Through the practice of silence, we tap into the boundless source of imagination, intuition, and innovation. We access the wisdom and inspiration that reside beyond the realm of words and external stimuli, connecting to the essence of our creative essence.

Let us honor the profound connection between silence and creativity. By embracing moments of stillness and creating intentional spaces for silence in our lives, we invite a deeper exploration of our creative potential. In the sanctuary of silence, we awaken our senses, listen to the whispers of our artistic spirit, and unleash our unique creative expression upon the world.

7.1 Discovering the Creative Potential Unlocked by Silence:

In the midst of our bustling lives, there lies a hidden treasure awaiting our discovery: the creative potential unlocked by silence. When we intentionally create space for silence, we open ourselves up to a world of untapped imagination, inspiration, and artistic expression.

In the gentle embrace of silence, our minds find respite from the noise of the external world. As the distractions fade away, a fertile ground emerges, allowing our creative thoughts to sprout and bloom. In this stillness, we uncover a wellspring of ideas, insights, and possibilities that have been patiently awaiting our attention.

Silence grants us the freedom to explore our thoughts, feelings, and innermost desires without judgment or interruption. It is within this sacred space that we dare to dream, allowing our imagination to wander unencumbered. We discover hidden connections, fresh perspectives, and novel approaches to creative challenges, unlocking new dimensions of our artistic potential.

As we immerse ourselves in the silence, we become attuned to the whispers of inspiration that arise from within. Ideas take shape with clarity, melodies form in our minds, and words dance across the page. We tap into a well of creativity that flows effortlessly, unearthing novel expressions of our unique artistic voice.

Silence serves as a nurturing cocoon for our creative ideas to incubate and evolve. It allows us to delve deeper into the depths of our artistic vision, honing our craft and refining our work with precision and authenticity. In the absence of external noise, we cultivate a heightened sense of focus and concentration, enabling us to channel our creative energy into meaningful and impactful endeavors.

By embracing the creative potential unlocked by silence, we honor the wisdom that resides within us. We learn to trust the intuitive nudges and spontaneous flashes of inspiration that emerge when we quiet the noise. As we continue to embrace moments of silence in our creative practice, we witness the transformative power of stillness, infusing our work with depth, originality, and a touch of magic.

Let us embark on the journey of discovering the creative potential unlocked by silence. By creating intentional spaces for silence and embracing the quietude within, we open ourselves to the vast universe of creativity that resides within our being. In the sanctuary of silence, we embrace the fullness of our artistic expression, allowing our creativity to flourish and leaving an indelible mark on the world.

7.2 Tapping into Inspiration and Innovation through Quiet Contemplation:

In the realm of inspiration and innovation, quiet contemplation becomes an invaluable gateway to unexplored realms of creativity. When we intentionally carve out moments of silence and immerse ourselves in quiet contemplation, we create a space for fresh insights, groundbreaking ideas, and transformative innovation to emerge.

During moments of quiet contemplation, we shift our focus inward, silencing the noise of external influences and distractions. In this stillness, our minds can wander freely, unhindered by the limitations of daily routines and preconceived notions. As we embrace the silence, we allow ourselves to be fully present, receptive to the subtle whispers of inspiration that arise from deep within our being.

Within the sanctuary of quiet contemplation, we tap into the wellspring of our imagination, unlocking a limitless source of ideas and possibilities. Freed from the constraints of time and external pressures, our minds engage in fluid and expansive thinking. We explore uncharted territories, make unlikely connections, and challenge conventional wisdom, paving the way for innovative breakthroughs.

In the sacred space of silence, our creativity is nourished and expanded. We listen to the subtle nuances of our thoughts, emotions, and intuitions, and find new pathways to express our unique perspectives. It is within this introspective state that we uncover the seeds of innovation, unearthing solutions to complex problems, and envisioning novel approaches that have the potential to change the world.

Quiet contemplation becomes a catalyst for deeper reflection and introspection, enabling us to gain clarity and a deeper understanding of our creative process. As we engage in stillness, we reflect upon our intentions, passions, and values, aligning them with our creative endeavors. Through this alignment, we infuse our work with purpose, authenticity, and a sense of meaning that resonates with others.

By regularly tapping into inspiration and innovation through quiet contemplation, we cultivate a mindset that embraces creativity as an integral part of our lives. We honor the transformative power of stillness, recognizing its role in sparking the innovative ideas that drive progress and change. With each moment of quiet contemplation, we strengthen our capacity to tap into the vast reservoir of inspiration that lies within us, leading us to create and innovate in ways that transcend our expectations.

Let us embrace the practice of quiet contemplation, allowing ourselves the gift of silence to fuel our imagination and foster innovation. As we tap into the depths of our inner wisdom, we awaken to a world of endless possibilities, where inspiration and innovation intertwine, creating a path of creativity that illuminates our lives and the lives of those around us.

Chapter 8: Silence and Inner Power

Within the profound depths of silence lies an extraordinary wellspring of inner power waiting to be discovered. When we embrace moments of silence, we access a reservoir of strength, resilience, and wisdom that resides within us. In the absence of external noise and distractions, we tap into the well of our true essence, connecting with the core of our being.

Silence serves as a sanctuary where we can retreat, finding solace and nourishment for our soul. As we immerse ourselves in the stillness, the noise of the outside world fades away, allowing us to listen to the gentle whispers of our inner voice. It is within this sacred silence that we reclaim our personal power, gaining a deep understanding of our values, passions, and purpose.

In the quietude of silence, we discover a profound sense of self-awareness and self-acceptance. We learn to embrace our strengths, acknowledge our weaknesses, and find empowerment in our vulnerabilities. Through silence, we connect with the authentic essence of who we truly are, untangling ourselves from societal expectations and external validation.

Silence becomes a source of inner strength, fostering a deep sense of resilience and self-confidence. As we cultivate the practice of silence, we develop the capacity to face life's challenges with grace and equanimity. The stillness within empowers us to navigate difficult circumstances, overcome obstacles, and tap into our innate abilities to adapt and grow.

Moreover, silence nourishes our inner wisdom, allowing us to access profound insights and clarity. In the absence of external influences, our intuition flourishes, guiding us towards aligned decisions and actions. The wisdom that arises in the silence becomes a guiding light, leading us towards choices that align with our highest potential and purpose.

In the sanctuary of silence, we connect with our inner power, tapping into a wellspring of strength, resilience, and wisdom that exists within each of us. By embracing moments of stillness, we honor the transformative potential of silence, allowing it to awaken our inner power and propel us forward on our journey of self-discovery and self-empowerment. Through the power of silence, we unleash our authentic selves, reclaim our personal power, and radiate our inner strength out into the world.

8.1 Unleashing Personal Power and Resilience through Silence:

Silence holds the key to unlocking our personal power and cultivating resilience in the face of life's challenges. When we embrace moments of silence, we tap into an inner wellspring of strength, courage, and unwavering determination. Within the depths of silence, we discover the transformative potential to unleash our true potential and build an unshakeable foundation of resilience.

In the sanctuary of silence, we create space for self-reflection and introspection, enabling us to connect with our authentic selves on a profound level. As we quiet the noise of external distractions, we tune into the wisdom that resides within us, gaining a deep understanding of our values, passions, and purpose. In this self-awareness, we find the source of our personal power—an unwavering connection to our inner truth and innate abilities.

Silence becomes a catalyst for self-empowerment. As we embrace the stillness, we shed the limiting beliefs and self-doubt that may have held us back. We reclaim our personal power by recognizing our strengths, embracing our unique qualities, and honoring the potential within us. Through this process, we awaken a sense of confidence, self-assurance, and the unwavering belief that we have the power to overcome any obstacle that comes our way.

Furthermore, silence nurtures resilience—a deep well of inner strength that allows us to bounce back from adversity with grace and determination. In the moments of quiet contemplation, we cultivate the capacity to stay centered amidst life's storms. We learn to navigate challenges with clarity, adaptability, and a steadfast mindset. In the face of setbacks, silence becomes a refuge, offering us the space to process emotions, regain balance, and tap into our reservoirs of resilience.

Through the practice of silence, we develop an unbreakable bond with our inner wisdom and intuition. The whispers of our intuition grow louder, guiding us towards aligned actions and decisions. In silence, we access the innate guidance that enables us to navigate life's complexities with grace and authenticity. We learn to trust ourselves, rely on our inner resources, and draw strength from the stillness within.

As we embrace moments of silence and weave them into our lives, we unleash our personal power and cultivate resilience that transcends challenges. The transformative potential of silence empowers us to step into our true selves, embrace our unique gifts, and overcome obstacles with unwavering strength. In the silence, we reclaim our personal power, nurture our resilience, and become the architects of our own destiny.

8.2 Connecting with Inner Strength and Authenticity:

Within the depths of our being, lies an innate wellspring of inner strength and authenticity waiting to be discovered. When we create moments of stillness and turn our attention inward, we connect with this wellspring, tapping into a source of unwavering power and a sense of genuine self. In these quiet moments, we shed the layers of external expectations and societal conditioning, embracing our true essence. Through this connection, we unlock the courage to live authentically, aligning our actions and choices with our deepest values. By nurturing this connection, we cultivate a profound sense of inner strength and authenticity that guides us on a path of fulfillment and purpose.

Chapter 9: Silence and Spiritual Connection

In the gentle embrace of silence, we open ourselves to the profound realm of spiritual connection. As we release the external noise and distractions, we create a sacred space where we can commune with the deepest parts of ourselves and the divine essence that permeates all existence. Within the stillness, we connect with a sense of presence, peace, and interconnectedness that transcends the limitations of the physical world.

In silence, we quiet the chatter of the mind, allowing the whispers of our soul to emerge. We become receptive to the subtle guidance, insights, and revelations that arise from within. It is in this receptive state that we deepen our spiritual connection, cultivating a sense of unity with something greater than ourselves. We tap into the universal energy that flows through us, recognizing our place in the interconnected web of life.

Silence becomes a sanctuary for spiritual exploration and contemplation. Through practices such as meditation, prayer, or quiet reflection, we embark on an inward journey of self-discovery and communion with the divine. We discover that in the depths of silence, we can transcend the boundaries of the ego and touch the vast expanse of our true nature. It is in this sacred stillness that we experience a profound sense of oneness, love, and wisdom.

Within the sanctuary of silence, we nourish our spiritual essence and deepen our connection to our inner divinity. We realize that spirituality is not confined to external rituals or beliefs, but rather a deeply personal and intimate experience that unfolds in the silence of our hearts. In silence, we find solace, guidance, and renewal, allowing us to navigate life's challenges with grace and surrender.

By embracing moments of silence and cultivating a regular practice of spiritual connection, we awaken to the transformative power of silence in our lives. We nurture our relationship with the divine, honoring the sacredness of our existence and fostering a deep sense of purpose and meaning. In the silence, we discover that we are not alone, but intricately woven into the tapestry of existence, connected to a higher consciousness that guides and supports us on our spiritual journey.

9.1 Deepening the Spiritual Journey through Silence and Contemplation:

In the sacred space of silence and contemplation, we embark on a profound journey of spiritual deepening and inner transformation. As we intentionally create moments of stillness, we invite a connection with the divine and dive into the depths of our spiritual essence.

Through silence, we quiet the external noise and distractions, allowing our inner voice to rise to the surface. In this receptive state, we attune ourselves to the subtle whispers of our soul, the guidance of higher realms, and the presence of a greater universal consciousness. We deepen our awareness of the sacredness of our existence and tap into the wisdom that lies beyond the realm of words and thoughts.

Contemplation becomes a gateway to exploring the mysteries of our being and the interconnectedness of all things. In the stillness, we reflect upon the profound questions of life, seeking deeper meaning and understanding. Through contemplative practices, such as meditation, reflection, or sacred rituals, we engage in a dialogue with our inner self, the divine, and the universal intelligence that permeates the cosmos.

As we embrace the practice of silence and contemplation, we peel back the layers of conditioning and ego, revealing the authentic essence of our spiritual nature. We come to know ourselves beyond the external roles and identities, uncovering the divine spark that resides within. In this deepening awareness, we align with our higher purpose and live in harmony with our truest self.

Silence and contemplation provide a sanctuary for nurturing our spiritual connection, nourishing our souls, and seeking communion with the divine. We discover that the richness of the spiritual journey lies not only in external practices but also in the deep introspection and stillness of our inner sanctuary. Through this sacred inner work, we cultivate qualities such as love, compassion, gratitude, and inner peace, which ripple outwards, transforming our lives and the world around us.

As we commit to the regular practice of silence and contemplation, we deepen our spiritual journey, fostering a profound sense of connection, meaning, and purpose. We awaken to the interplay of the seen and unseen, recognizing that our existence is part of a greater tapestry of divine unfolding. In the stillness, we find solace, guidance, and profound wisdom, supporting us as we navigate the complexities of life and embark on a transformative spiritual odyssey.

9.2 Nurturing a Connection with the Divine and Higher Consciousness:

Nurturing a deep and sacred connection with the divine and higher consciousness is a transformative journey that unfolds through intentional practices of silence, reflection, and spiritual devotion. As we create space for stillness and turn our attention inward, we open ourselves to the vastness of the divine presence that resides within and around us. Through prayer, meditation, or heartfelt contemplation, we invite a profound communion with the universal intelligence and tap into the infinite wisdom, love, and guidance that flows from higher realms. In nurturing this connection, we awaken to our interconnectedness with all of creation, expand our awareness, and align our lives with divine purpose, experiencing a sense of profound unity, inner peace, and spiritual fulfillment.

C*onclusion*

- **Embracing the Power Within:**

In conclusion, embracing the power within is the gateway to unlocking our true potential and living a life of authenticity, purpose, and fulfillment. Through silence and mindfulness, we cultivate self-awareness, emotional well-being, and resilience. By harnessing the therapeutic aspects of silence, we tap into our inner wisdom and discover the transformative power of stillness. Connecting with our intuition, we make decisions aligned with our true selves and navigate life's challenges with grace and trust. Silence becomes a catalyst for creativity, inspiration, and innovation, allowing us to express our unique gifts and make a meaningful impact in the world. Moreover, in the sacred space of silence, we deepen our spiritual connection, nurturing a profound sense of unity, inner peace, and alignment with the divine. By embracing the power within, we embark on a lifelong journey of self-discovery, self-empowerment, and the realization of our highest potential.